W9-BGU-481

DATE DUE

Published by Creative Education
123 South Broad Street, Mankato, Minnesota 56001
Creative Education is an imprint of The Creative Company

Designed by Stephanie Blumenthal

Photographs by Gene Ahrens, Archive Photos, Frank Balthis,
James Blank, Richard Cummins, Don Eastman, Priscilla Eastman,
Bruce Hemmeon, Gunter Marx, Richard Nowitz, Photri, James Rowan

Library of Congress Cataloging-in-Publication Data

Iverson, Carol.
Houses / by Carol Iverson.
p. cm. — (Designing the future)
Includes index.
ISBN 1-58341-187-9
1. Dwellings—Juvenile literature.
[1. Dwellings.] I. Title. II. Series.
GT172 .I84   2001
392.3'6—dc21   00-064472

First Edition

9 8 7 6 5 4 3 2 1

Cover, colonial-era stone house;
p. 1, Belvedere House, Galena, Illinois;
p. 2, Victorian row houses;
p. 3, historic home in the
Canadian Yukon

HOUSES

CAROL IVERSON

CREATIVE C EDUCATION

A house serves many purposes. It provides people with a place to eat and sleep, and it provides families with a place to grow and share their lives with one another. It offers shelter from bad weather, animals, and intruders.

The way people live affects the kinds of homes they build, and when their lifestyles change, they create houses that better suit their new ways of living. People who live under the constant threat of attack by hostile enemies will build houses that offer them protection.

Log cabin in Wyoming

A 200-year-old Icelandic home

The natural resources available to people and their society's level of technology also affect house design. People who live near forests are most likely to build with wood. Where wood is scarce, people may use stone, brick, or sod. In industrialized societies, people may build with steel, or use heavy machinery instead of hand tools to construct their houses.

People who value hospitality will build houses that have space to entertain guests. People who have to survive cold winters will build the warmest houses they can, and people who face hot summers will build the coolest houses they can.

The houses people are able to build will also affect the lives they lead. For example, when many people share a small space, each person will have little privacy. If they become able to build a larger house, they may begin to expect a new level of privacy.

Carson House, Eureka, California

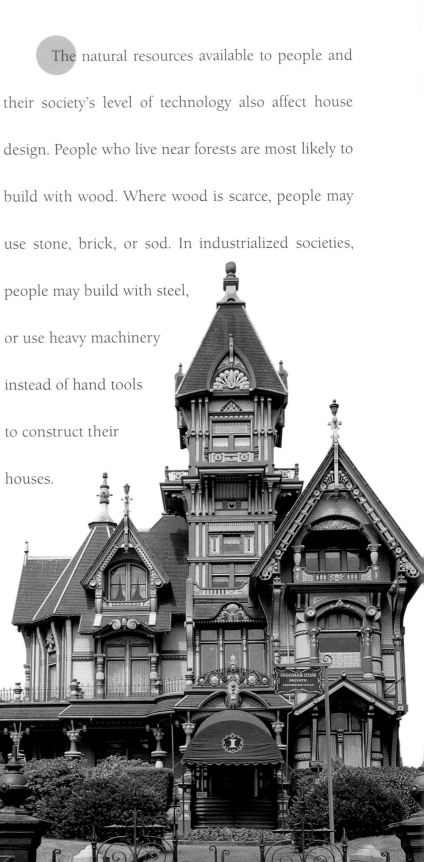

The Taos Pueblo, New Mexico

The Pueblo Indian ruins of Mesa Verde, Colorado

Building the earliest houses required few tools, if any. Cave dwellings have been found in many parts of the world, including North and South America, Europe, and Asia. The people who lived in them carved their homes out of rock, often to provide protection from invaders. The soil in many cave dwelling areas contains volcanic ash and dust, making it relatively easy to carve.

In some places, shelves, beds, and stools were also carved out of rock. People often think that only prehistoric people lived in caves, but in many places caves were used well into the 20th century. In some villages in Romania and China, cave dwellings are still in use.

Historically, houses reflect the time, place, and culture in which they were built. Over the course of human history, the range of places that human beings have called home is incredible.

> **N**ear Moscow, archeologists unearthed a 22,000-year-old settlement that was once inhabited by Stone-Age people who hunted woolly mammoths. The archeologists found two round dwellings with roofs made from mammoth bones.

Carved cave dwellings in Turkey

Towers were often built for protection and extra ventilation

Beginning in the third century, in Yemen, a small country in the Middle East, tower houses were built, and some are still standing. The basic feature of this house was its sound, tall design. The rooms were placed one above the other, with only one room on each floor. A central staircase rose through the house. Yemen's tower houses were made of stone or brick, and most were from five to nine stories high. Thick outside walls kept the occupants cool during warm days and warm on cool nights. The ground floor, which had no windows, was a place for animals, grain, and storage. The second floor was a living area. The third floor was reserved for special occasions and celebrations. The remaining floors held the kitchen and other living spaces. The

In Korea, around the middle of the seventh century, a law dictated the size of house a person could build. The higher a person placed in society, the larger his house could be.

top floor often served as a place for men to hold social gatherings.

Many hundreds of years later, in the 15th century, people in power built tower houses far away from Yemen, in Ireland. The Irish tower houses were square, and some had an opening above the door through which the occupants could drop rocks or boiling water on attackers. These houses were built like fortresses.

Blockhouses were used mainly by military troops

These old Swiss houses offered little privacy

comfort, and tapestries hung on the walls not only for decoration but also for protection from the cold. Privacy was a luxury here, too. These residences were often full of people, including friends and people who worked for the home's owners.

During this period in history, most common-folks' houses were small. Many of them had no more than one room, so there was no privacy. By the 17th century, however, many European houses became larger, and since more rooms were available, privacy became more common.

When people moved from Europe to America, they developed another method of building houses. Sod, bricks of grass-covered soil, quickly became a popular building

Well-off tradespeople of the Middle Ages built family homes, not fortresses. The main floor often served as a shop and work area. The second floor was commonly used for cooking, eating, sleeping, and entertaining. Normally, this area was sparsely furnished. A chest, for example, might be used for both seating and storage. These houses offered little

Pit fireplaces without chimneys have been used since ancient times, but they create a lot of smoke. The chimney came into use in Europe in the 11th century, but it wasn't until the 12th century that the chimney was extended high enough above the roof to draw the smoke out of the house.

A one-room cottage with stone shingles

material. Sod houses were commonly built during the 19th century on the Great Plains of the United States, where trees were scarce and sod was readily available. Sod blocks made excellent insulation, and they were fireproof. The floor of a "soddie" was usually dirt, and the windows were covered with greased paper or animal skins. Sod houses had the disadvantage of being attractive to bugs,

In some parts of the world, cracks and small openings in huts are sealed and mortared with animal droppings, or dung. Entire huts, including the walls and roof, can be made of dung.

snakes, and mice. In spite of this, some sod houses were inhabited as late as the 1950s.

There was no typical sod house. Each was built by its owners to fit their particular needs. Many were dug into hillsides, so they were partially underground. This helped insulate them. The quality of construction depended on the expertise of the builder. Some sod houses

Sod houses tucked into the countryside

An Irish crannog set in a grassy marsh

stood for decades, while others deteriorated rapidly.

Some people live not on land, but on water. In Ireland and Scotland, crannogs were built as early as 4000 B.C. to protect their inhabitants from enemies. These settlements were constructed upon natural islands or man-made wooden platforms set in lakes, marshes, rivers, or swamps. Most were either circular or oval and measured 16 to 34 yards (15–30 m) in diameter. Round huts were built on top of the base

and surrounded by a fence. A set of stepping stones, called a causeway, was laid just under the water, linking the crannog to dry land. Frequently, a curve or angle was built into the causeway to trick unwelcome callers. Only the people who lived there knew where the stepping stones were. Crannogs were inhabited until the 17th century, when the invention of gunpowder reduced their effectiveness as safe havens.

Lake and river houses may also float on the

water. Houseboats are found on lakes and rivers in many parts of the world, including the Americas, Europe, Asia, and the South Pacific. In Asia, houseboats are called sampans, or "junks." This type of house has been in use for centuries. These boats are equipped with oars, sails, and sometimes motors, and have a sleeping cabin at one end. In the year 2000, as many as 6,000 people lived and worked on junks in the Hong Kong harbor, fishing, giving tours of the harbor, and working as garbage collectors.

A typical junk floating in a Hong Kong harbor

Traditional Japanese houses have movable walls called shoji (SHOW-jee) screens. These are panels framed by wooden strips and covered with thin, almost transparent paper. The screens can be moved to create small private spaces, such as bedrooms, or larger open ones, such as dining rooms. Paper doors called fusuma (foo-SOO-may) are also used. These are light, sliding partitions covered with thick paper and mounted in grooves on the floor and ceiling so they can slide open or closed.

In Beijing, China, the traditional upper-class household consisted of a square compound made of four houses built around an inner courtyard. The main house was for the most important members of the family, which included the elders. It was always built so that it faced south. The size of the inner courtyard depended on the wealth

Gassho-style farmhouse in Japan

The graceful curve of a Chinese roof

of the owner. Large compounds could have as many as three inner courtyards. Today, these traditional compounds are less common than relatively modern residential buildings.

Designs or symbols adorn the doorposts of many Chinese houses. When a bat, which rhymes with the Mandarin word for luck, accompanies

Some homeless people make shelters out of whatever they can find—things such as cardboard boxes, scrap lumber, and discarded windows. Even though these shelters may be crudely built, they can provide some protection from the elements.

a sign for longevity, the design expresses the hope for good luck and a long life for the inhabitants.

The distinct roofing style used throughout China hasn't changed in centuries. The eaves and corners of many roofs curl gracefully upward. The style originally came from Buddhist temples and was intended to fend

off evil spirits, which were believed to travel in straight lines. The sidewalks leading to houses are often crooked for this same reason.

Tree houses were common in the South Pacific and Southeast Asia. In New Guinea, tree houses were used as fortresses. When a village came under attack, the residents would climb into the tree houses and pull the ladders up behind them. If the attackers tried to

CHINESE CULTURE

In northern China, most houses are built facing exactly north, exactly south, exactly east, or exactly west.

The Tiger Pagoda, Hong Kong

Chinese buildings today still reflect traditional Buddhist beliefs

chop the tree down, the villagers threw stones and spears at them.

In what is now Mongolia, people often lived in large tents called gers. A ger was circular and had a wooden frame covered with felt made from yak hair. Designed by nomads, people who moved from place to place, it was well suited to the way they lived. One person could set up the ger in an hour, and it could survive rain and snowstorms. The door was small

"Green building" is the term used for construction that recycles, reduces material use, and saves water and energy. The goal of green building is to make houses more environmentally friendly than they would otherwise be.

and close to the earth, keeping the heat inside. Large openings in the roof let the smoke out, and the sides could be partially raised to provide ventilation. These tents were also called yurts, which comes from a Turkish word. Today, all around the world, people still use tents designed like gers.

The Australian Aborigines—the original people of Australia—are also nomads. They developed a dwelling called a gunyah, a word that means "little

An Australian Aborigine gunyah

Turkish tent well-suited for a nomadic lifestyle

Octagonal house with a large, ornate cupola

house." Gunyahs are big enough to hold only three or four people but are sturdy enough to withstand wind and rain. They are made of large branches, boughs, twigs, leaves, and bark. Inside, the occupants sit and sleep on sand or grass. In the summer, they sleep outside, beside campfires. Gunyahs are temporary shelters that can be left behind because they cost nothing to build; another one can be constructed anywhere trees are found.

Octagonal houses were built in many parts of the United States in the 1800s. Instead of the conventional four sides, the octagonal house had eight, and it could be from one to five stories tall. In addition to traditional windows, it had a cupola, or tower room, at the top of the house. This provided additional lighting and an excellent view of

There is such a thing as a glass house. Single-family homes made from glass, held together with metal and topped by conventional roofs, exist in the United States, Chile, and Japan.

24

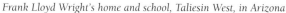

the surrounding landscape. In *The Octagon House: A Home for All*, Oscar Fowler asked, "Why so little progress in architecture when there is so much in other matters? Why not take our pattern from nature? Her forms are most spherical." He believed the octagonal house was more conducive to better health than the conventional four-sided home, since it allowed for more sunlight and better ventilation.

Perhaps the most influential architect to take his cue from nature was Frank Lloyd Wright. A pioneer in the modern style of housing, Wright created the philosophy of "organic architecture." This philosophy maintains that a building should develop out of its natural surroundings. Such ideals led to the construction of some of the most famous houses of the 20th century, including Fallingwater and Taliesin West.

Frank Lloyd Wright's home and school, Taliesin West, in Arizona

Frank Lloyd Wright's Fallingwater house in Pennsylvania

The Monsanto House of the Future, Disneyland, California

Today, many people around the world are taking the ideas introduced by Wright and expanding them. Earth-sheltered homes are an example of this. This method of construction blends technologies of the present, such as solar energy, with the earth-sheltered sod house tradition used by people in the past.

Visitors to Pigeon Cove, Massachusetts, can see a small house made almost entirely of newspaper—even the furnishings. A roof of tar and shingles covers it, protecting it from the elements. No one lives in the house, but it is a tourist attraction.

Yet attempting to reconnect with nature was by no means the only trend in housing architecture during the 20th century. In California in 1957, Disneyland built the Monsanto House of the Future out of plastics. The house featured what were then considered futuristic items such as microwave ovens, picture telephones,

Floating river houses in British Columbia, Canada

electric toothbrushes, and plastic furniture. Most of those things are now common.

What does today's house of the future look like? Some architects say that in the future most houses will look like they do now, but the technology inside and out will change. Microwave clothes dryers may be common and a robot mower might cut the lawn. As for the structure itself, builders may make

NONTRADITIONAL HOMES

People often convert structures that are not houses into dwellings. Houses have been made out of railroad cars and cabooses, churches, schools, barns, silos, and windmills.

Tomorrow's homes may borrow from past styles

A lighthouse on the shore of Lake Michigan

An Egyptian house built with readily available materials

greater use of recycled and composite materials that are stronger, lighter, and cheaper than traditional wood, resulting in the cutting of fewer trees.

Around the world and throughout human history, people have built their houses out of the materials that were available. From those materials, they have built houses to meet their particular needs. The resourcefulness of the world's people is reflected in the variety of homes they have built—and in the variety of homes they will continue to build.

INDEX